SIX FIGURE TEENS

Make Six Figures Before Your 21st Birthday

TABLE OF CONTENTS

Introduction

As a young child, you can become aware of the nuances of entrepreneurship and begin the process of starting your own business. Kids should be able to incorporate standard business practices as part of their growth process, and as you continue to absorb the world around you, these methods will be more relatable. As little as the age of five, children will start to comprehend business theories. As you become aware of the businesses around, you'll begin to raise questions and demonstrate an interest to build on. The more kids advance in age, the more they start to recognize business and the significance of entrepreneurship in society and fix it as part of their futures. Regardless of your age, if you have a positive attitude towards learning, you are old enough to know about entrepreneurship. If you can read and desire to learn about business, you can gain a lot from this book. There is no reason to rush to learn about entrepreneurship and no pressure, but the sooner you develop the understanding. The sooner you will have the confidence to talk about business and finally start up a venture.

As you develop skills and acquire knowledge from reading this book, you will cultivate abilities to assist you in school and your day-to-day operations. By absorbing this information, it will expand the way you view the world compared to your peers. This pertains to many skills that you will begin to acquire as you think about and learn about business. It is important to note that a small business with just a few customers tends to treat every customer differently, providing a high level of personal and personalized service. Nonetheless, as the business matures and gains more customers, making a profit while delivering such a highly personalized service becomes hard. For example, let's take a look at your local ice cream shop. When they first open for business, they may know each person by name and spend time talking with each customer. However, as the business grows, the owner will have to service more customers and won't spend as much time with specific customers.

Chapter 1: Choosing A Business

Owning a business involves working flexible hours and not being accountable to a manager or employee. Being able to make your own decisions, and, in effect, having complete autonomy or control over your business. You must remember that just because you have this much autonomy, it is even more vital that you hold yourself accountable daily. Freedom with their schedule is one of the main things that cause entrepreneurs to fail. Most people don't have the discipline to commit and maintain a schedule when someone isn't looking over their shoulder.

Choose A Business That You Are Passionate About

When choosing which business you want to start, make sure you consider the things you care about the most. While some kids are interested in activities like music, dance, sports, others might start their own business. Everyone is different, and as a result of these differences, ten kids put together in a room will probably not have the same passion for a particular thing, which is why you should never force yourself to start a business that you're don't like.

In fourth grade, I can still remember when my entire class drew a picture of what they wanted to be when they grew up. I drew a picture of a man in a suit that was standing in front of a building. Underneath the drawing, I wrote "Entrepreneur"; I no longer have the picture. But I wonder if I even spelled the word right. I didn't know what kind of business I wanted to start, but I knew that I wanted to be a business owner

Try to help adults see your vision. The most effective method to determine the kind of business **that** is good for you is to motivate yourself to follow your passions. If you notice that you can perform in an area you like, seek assistance in finding out more in that area.

When I was a kid, I like collecting baseball cards. And I remember going to a garage sale one day, and I bought a box full of baseball cards for $1. In that box was a rookie card of Hall Of Famer David Robinson. I quickly went to the store where they bought and sold cards and sold that card for $10. I was probably taken advantage of by the store owner, but I made a 1,000% profit. So why did I care? At the writing of this book, that same card is worth an average of $650. I held on to that card, or let's say I took that same strategy and went to more garage sales and bought more boxes of cards for cheap and sold them too; in today's world, that's called retail arbitrage.

What Are Your Natural Gifts
As a kid, what shows up naturally to you is always a blessing in the form of a gift. Understanding your natural gifts can be extremely useful in starting up your own business. Pay attention to the things that people say that you do well. The closer your work aligns with your character and natural proficiency, the more enjoyment and accomplishment you will have when you start your business. You're lucky enough to be on this journey at an early age. Most adults had long forgotten the dreams they had when they were younger. That is why your parents will tell you to enjoy being a kid.

Ask an adult to help you unlock your hidden potentials. The key is to find often hidden abilities in yourself. These abilities could contribute to business success or engage you in learning about your interests and developing your natural abilities. You can ask your parents to nurture your gifts and abilities and help build skills and future opportunities. If kids engage in what they are good at, they will develop confidence, which will spread to other activities and personal development. As a child, I wasn't particularly good at sports. But I was great at public speaking and good at asking questions and interviewing people. Now, as an adult, I'm using those gifts to help other people, such as yourself, achieve their dreams.

What Businesses Do You Find The Most Interesting?
Think of things you already know how to do, want to learn to do, or simply enjoy. Profitable businesses exist in all industries, and you can do the same if the circumstances are right. This can be done by either teaching others how to do it, packaging and selling a product, or selling related products to fellow enthusiasts. Doing something enjoyable is an excellent way to ignite commitment and possibly uncover an idea that will prove profitable to you. What skill do you have that you can teach others?

Why are you going into business?
Having a business can educate you on responsibilities and better understand how money is used in society. Also, maintaining a business is a considerable means for children to

concentrate their power and efforts on something helpful rather than just sitting around the house.

Opening a business as a child can be rewarding in many ways. You can discover crucial business techniques, improve your math mastery, impress your parents and accumulate some capital (otherwise known as money) -- all at the same time. The following are some of the reasons a kid should go into business.

1. All kids will grow up to be involved in a business. You'll eventually work in a company at a job or interact with a business as a consumer and customer.

2. Business affects everyone; therefore, it is one of the most relevant things to learn about.

3. Business helps kids reach their potential. Learning about business will help you succeed in whatever path you choose in life. For example, I recommend every young person try their hands at a sales job. It will teach you perseverance and help you deal with rejection. Rejection is a natural part of life, especially for anyone that wants to achieve more in life.

4. Owning a business can help with self-esteem. - Engaging in business demonstrates respect for their intelligence and potential. Also, gaining respect from adults builds kids' confidence, which leads to them taking on responsibility and

learning from new opportunities. Elevated confidence will contribute significantly to child development. Once you realize you can do something, you will embrace the learning and development of the business's systems and processes.

5. Why not? Some adults feel that there is a risk of putting too much pressure on kids. Learning about business can help you manage stress or responsibility. Such as creating a business mindset and the skills necessary for business. Kids are spending increasing amounts of time on the internet, cell phones, video games, and social networking, all of which have pros and cons. One pro is that people of all ages make money using the same devices we use in everyday life.

Who will benefit from your business?
The person that will benefit from a kid owned business most is the kid. The benefit is more long term because the knowledge acquired from an entrepreneur's mindset will pave the way to manage companies and jobs when fully grown. Most successful entrepreneurs, including myself, failed at the first attempts at starting a business. As people get older, they can't afford to take certain risks. So it's best to get those learning experiences out the way early.

Who Is Your Target Customer
To market your product or service, you must modify your marketing and sales efforts to reach the section of the population that will most likely buy your product or service. It

is critical that you identify your primary market; so that you can use your resources efficiently. If you don't know who your customers are, how will you be able to assess whether you are meeting their needs? Since success depends on your ability to meet customers' needs and desires, you must know who your customers are, what they want, where they live, and what they can afford. You need to identify your target customer before you understand their needs and how to fulfill them.

How will you differentiate yourself from other businesses
Considering some plans will direct your awareness and assist you with determining the future for your business. You'll need to compare your business to your competitors.

Where do you perform best?
What renders you different?
What can your business do better than any other company?

Solving these issues will enable you to develop a picture of your company and where it is headed.

Help Yourself Invest In Learning More About Their Industry
You have to learn the basics, the procedures of the business to develop. You should examine business-training programs as a way to learn about business and to develop the necessary skills. Ask an adult about training that can be explained to kids. Kids must learn to operate their business and push themselves to

improve to be the best they can. Running a business is an important undertaking at any age. An adult can take some time to help you with research, preparation, and strategies before getting started. A business club for kids is a great chance to put together or join to explore entrepreneurship with friends. Youtube University is the best source for learning a new skill. I wish I had Youtube when I was a kid. You'll find thousands of videos about any topic by simply entering it in the search bar. Make sure to get your parent's permission before doing so.

Chapter 2: Setting Goals And Formulating A Business Plan

SETTING GOALS

Successful entrepreneurs are intensely goal-oriented. They always achieve more than those without goals. They know what they want and are focused on getting it done every day. Ask parents for help with setting your goals and agree as a family what you can achieve. Prioritize goals according to their importance to you and your family. Goals will ultimately differ in the length of time needed to achieve them. So, the time required to accomplish one goal will be different from the time necessary to achieve another. It can be overwhelming to start working on all goals in the same year. I've noticed the best way to accomplish a big goal is to break it down into small chunks.

Let's say you have a goal of waking up an hour earlier every morning to work on your business. Instead of saying you'll wake up an hour earlier tomorrow, set a goal to wake up 15 minutes earlier tomorrow. Next week, set a goal to wake up another 15 minutes earlier (a total of 30 minutes earlier). The week after that, wake up 15 minutes earlier (a total of 45 minutes earlier). The week after that, wake up another 15 minutes earlier (a total of one hour earlier). Once this goal is accomplished, you can work on another goal. If you work on one goal a month, you'll achieve 12 goals a year. That's impressive! While it may seem silly to take a whole month to accomplish a goal that can be done in one day. It's best to focus on creating a consistent habit of waking up earlier. The same can be said for saving money!

Goals must be specific and concise, and it's essential to write your goals down. The funny thing about the way our brain works; is that when you write something down, the world finds a way to bring those things into your life. It's called the Reticular Activating System (RAS). The RAS blocks out insignificant things from your consciousness; so that your you, your body, and your brain don't get overwhelmed. Here are two examples of the RAS at work:

1.) You didn't notice the feeling in your left foot until I said your left foot
2.) When you or your parents get a new car, you'll automatically see that car more often when driving around time.
3.) Hearing a phrase or the name of a person for the first time one day, and out of nowhere, you naturally see that phrase or name more often

The same goes for when you set goals. By setting your mind to something, the law of attraction will eventually bring people's necessary things in your life for you to accomplish that goal. The law of attraction was at work when I bought that David Robinson rookie card. I had such a love for sports cards that I knew I would eventually find a valuable one. Some people will call that luck, but luck is what happens when opportunity meets preparation.

A goal is a target toward which you can direct your efforts. Without a plan, you are bound to drift in the wrong direction, thus wasting time and effort. Your school or local sports teams have a goal to win a game or the championship. To reach this goal, they have to practice honing (meaning to get better) their skills. Your goal should be specific and have a deadline; a goal without a deadline is a wish.

> A wish: I want to save money
> A goal: I want to save $100 by the end of the summer

> A wish: I will start a business
> A goal: I will start a business by the end of the year

> A wish: I will wake up earlier
> A goal: I will wake up one hour earlier by the end of the month

You need to formulate a clear notion of what you want in life and why you want it. It's the goal that establishes the deep-seated, almost blind faith that things will work out all right if you keep going. Most people have goals they're working on right now, even if they didn't officially set them. A goal is simply something you want to complete or accomplish by a deadline. A goal can be something you want to achieve today, this week, this month, throughout the entire year, or at some point in your lifetime. When you think of goals, you may think of larger things, maybe seemingly unattainable things. Almost anything can be a goal if it' s important to you that you accomplish it. You may also see New Year's resolutions as goals, which is another way to frame this basic concept. A good exercise would be to have a goal-setting time with your friends and family.

Goals Must Be Brought To Life

Goals set the direction, the distance, the pace, and the point of completion. In sports, the goal is clear, and the coaches use strategies to achieve it. Great coaches adapt game plans to adjust to changing conditions. While continually keeping their eye on the ultimate goal, which is winning. As with all good teams, they have the determination to overcome obstacles and adversity and are willing to pay the price for victory. Setting and reaching goals is a fundamental part of winning in business and life. Whatever personal goals you place in your subconscious mind, your mind begins to work night and day to achieve them. When you have a long list of goals you'd like to achieve, you have more to strive for; and more opportunities to check those goals off your list. When you reach a goal, you should check that goal off your list. And the satisfaction you feel every time you check one of those goals off your list; will inspire you to achieve more goals. It's also important to reward yourself when you accomplish a goal. Appreciate the small victories to avoid losing momentum. The small victories inevitably lead to big wins. Make a list of the goals you'd like to achieve in different periods of your life, some goals you want to accomplish in a year, and others you want to accomplish in the next two years. Be as specific as possible about it. Make sure you include all the details like:

When it will happen
Where you want it to happen
How much you want to make
A specific thing you want to buy
What help from others will you need to accomplish it
What will you need to learn to accomplish it
How many customers do you want to have
How many products you want to sell

And so on, keep your goals somewhere close so that you can review them daily. This is where a notebook is useful. Your goals can be written in a journal next to your bed, on your wall, or a bathroom mirror. {Remember to ask your parents first}

Write your goals down in **a journal** for easy access, where you can shuffle through it every morning. You can also write it on a poster or piece of paper you hang on the wall beside your computer or tablet. Make sure you read your **goals** each night before you fall asleep. Doing this will keep them at the forefront of your mind; you'll be more likely to make them a reality. Every time you check a goal off your list, make sure you reward yourself. Writing your goals This will significantly increase your chances of success. The same is true when you don't take action, goals and plans become nothing.

Writing A Business Plan

Your business plan is the foundation of your business. It's a roadmap for how to structure, run, and grow your new venture. You'll use it to persuade people that working with you — or investing in your company — is a smart choice. There's no right or wrong way to make a business plan. A business plan provides you with a comprehensive overview of all the aspects of your business.

This overview is the foundation of your business—the underlying structure that provides the basis of your entire operation. Prepared in advance, a business plan allows you to review the pros and cons of your proposed business before you make a financial and emotional commitment to it. A prospective business owner and those already in business need to develop a written plan. Written plans provide a management tool for determining an idea's specific strengths and weaknesses, documenting reasonable objectives, and identifying resources to attain them. It's also important to look at the blueprint of people and businesses that are currently successful. Success leaves clues and taking the time to watch Youtube videos. Or possibly paying for a course from a reputable source could save you millions and time as well.

A written plan will also provide the basis for developing a more detailed business operating plan. The risk of starting a business cannot be eliminated, but a good business plan will reduce the risk. A well-constructed business plan is the foundation of a profitable organization. A good business plan will act as a guide by starting and managing a business. A business plan proves awareness comprehensive, clarified outline of all the qualities of your business. This outline is the blueprint of your business—the underlying system that delivers this awareness of your entire operation. It allows you to review your business's merits before making a financial and personal allegiance to it.

Your business plan will help you recognize your areas of strength and weakness. You can assess business needs that would otherwise be ignored.

Your business plan should include your target audience, what competition exists, expected start-up and ongoing costs, and when the business is likely to be profitable.

This plan should include such things as:

> Where will you run your business?
> How much will it cost to operate?
> What will your schedule look like?
> How much money you'll need to get started?

Seeing your plan in writing helps to remind you about what actions are necessary to reach your goals. It helps to check your progress quicker than relying on memory alone. Your business plan should include:

Where will you run your business?

Who will your customers be? (e.g., adults, other kids or teens, men, women, people with dogs, people who own their homes, etc.)

What supplies, tools, and equipment will you need?

Where will you get those things, and how much do they cost?

How much money will you need to get started and to run your business until the money comes in from your customers?

How much will you charge for your products or services?

What will you call your business?

How will you advertise your business?

As a kid, you must be able to write down your goals and business plans; and write down the expenses of all the things you'll need to start.

What Help Will You Need From Your Parent or Guardian?
Express your interest in starting a business; they can offer valuable guidance and feedback as you decide on the path you'll take. Parents can help you brainstorm ideas and take inventory of your skills and talents. Their insight will also prove helpful in ruling out businesses that have high barriers to entry, which will demand excessive time or come with extensive liability ramifications. Parents can help you stay focused on your ideas and the tasks ahead.

Adults have many life experiences that can help you succeed in the early stages to experience the feeling of success, which will motivate you to set higher goals going forward. Many children determine their success based on the expectations of parents and adults they respect. Parents' expectations affect what children learn and how successful they are. They can help you stay realistic and help to set obtainable goals to build confidence. Allow yourself room to succeed on your terms. It doesn't matter whether you ask your parents for help or not, one thing you should expect is that they will indeed offer their support, and once they do, it is essential for you to accept it. Suppose you find that you don't have these types of role models in your life. You can go online and look for mentorship programs; books are a great way to have a mentor. A book accumulated knowledge of someone you'll probably never meet in person. For example, I spent close to thirty years gaining the know-how; that I eventually wrote in this book's pages.

How Much Money Do You Need To Invest?
Most businesses require at least some initial investment up front. You may need the help of your parent as they may be a significant investor. But don't fall for the myth that you need a lot of money to start a business. I have started companies with a lot of money, and I've started companies with little to no money. There is so much involved in a new business; having a steady stream of cash can be detrimental. Having little or no money will allow you to take the slow and steady approach. At the same time, you are learning the nuances of the business.

Having money won't be a determining factor in the success or viability of your company.

Furthermore, just as many businesses have failed with no money, others with tons of capital failed. If you've been earning an allowance or working part-time for a company in your area, you may have some money saved. Will that be enough to start your business and keep it afloat until customers' revenue starts flowing? If not, you may want to ask your parents if there are additional chores you can do at home to earn some extra cash, seek a temporary weekend job, or ask friends and family members if they are willing to loan you money. There also tons of side jobs that you can do online to create capital for your company. If you borrow money from a family member, consider working out a repayment plan to give yourself the real-life experience with borrowing money from a lender and paying it back. Many useful products and business ideas never start because of the difficulties associated with securing financing. Many businesses start but fail because of a lack of funding. Financing is an area that all business operators need to spend time on and understand. Finance relates to the money aspects of your business—the practice of obtaining and managing money. Finance includes the capital involved in a project, especially the capital needed to start a new business. You now realize there are many steps to take to develop a business. Often these steps require money the company might not have. A business needs financing when it doesn't have the money it requires in the bank or does not take in enough revenue to keep the business afloat. This funding can come from a person, bank, company, or investor. This money can be in the form of borrowing or capital. Borrowing means you use other people's money with the intent of paying it back while you pay interest, which is the cost of borrowing the money.

What Skills Will You Need To Acquire To Start Your Business?

If you want to start your own business, you need to learn the specific skills that underpin these qualities. You can learn life skills to prepare for business at any age. Skills, such as learning to have a professional conversation or learning a new language(s). Are examples of life skills that are learned and applicable to business; they contribute to creating the foundation for other skills. New skills can be learned at all stages of life and will make you more independent and marketable. Marketable is the ability to have skill sets that you can bring to the market (public or employees); in exchange for a benefit (usually a monetary benefit). Life skill prepares you for a successful future in business. Also, skill development builds other skills. These life skills build confidence, which encourages your ability and aptitude to develop skills further.

Running a business is a demanding task. Seek assistance if you are unsure about your abilities and skills. Developing the necessary skills will provide your business with a solid foundation. You will require several skills to start and run a business. It is essential to identify what skills you need to develop or improve to succeed in your day-to-day business operations.

These are the essential business skills:

1. Financial management

Managing your finances is critical. Over time, you will need to forecast your cash flow, sales, and calculate your profit and loss statements. Possessing sound financial management techniques will enable you to operate your business profitably and safeguard your financial investment. Even if you haven't earned a dollar in your business, having these procedures in place at your enterprise's start will put you lightyears ahead of most entrepreneurs.

2. Marketing, Sales, and Customer Service

It is essential to be able to market your products or services effectively. Providing good customer service and having a marketing strategy in place will benefit you in generating sales. You have to know who your customer is, and why that customer buys —Google' how to learn copywriting' to communicate how to communicate with your target market. Copywriting can be a great business too! People spend millions of dollars to Copywrite for companies. Think of your favorite commercial; a copywriter laid out specific phrases and sentences that compelled you to like that product.

3. Communication and negotiation

You will need to communicate and negotiate with your suppliers, potential investors, customers, and employees. Having effective written and verbal communication skills will help you to build good working relationships. Every communication should reflect the image you are trying to project.

4. Leadership

If you employ people, leadership will be a crucial skill. You must be able to motivate your staff to get the best out of them and improve productivity. Allocate time to mentor and coach your employees. Don't confuse leadership with being mean, disrespectful, or rude. Good leaders are great communicators and are firm with their standards. Great leaders lead by example!

5. Project management and planning

Starting a business means you will have to manage a range of projects, such as setting up a website, arranging the build-out of your premises, and developing a range of policies and procedures. Knowing how to effectively manage your resources of time, money, and support team will help you achieve your goals.

6. Delegation and time management

Failure to delegate is a trap many business owners fall into because they are reluctant to let go of control. Managing your time effectively may mean delegating responsibility to someone else in the business or outsourcing the task. Identifying who you can delegate tasks to allows you to concentrate on those tasks that generate revenue. You'll also need to have an understanding of your strengths and weaknesses. Focus on your strengths and delegate your weaknesses to people who exhibit strength in areas in which you exhibit weaknesses.

7. Problem solving

However, much you plan, you will encounter problems in your business. This means you need to have good decision making and problem-solving skills under pressure.

8. Networking

Building good relationships through networking will help you grow your business and give you the support you'll need. Consider joining an industry or business association to expand your network. Your network is your net worth. People do business with people that they know, like, and trust. The most important part about that equation is the "knowing." You can have the best product or service in the world. But, if no one knows about you, you won't sell anything. Sometimes, people get the sale simply because they were in the right room at the right time. Or someone that knew you were in the right room at the right time; and spoke highly of you.

How Much Time Do You Think It'll Take To Make The Business Profitable?

It is natural to wonder how long it will take before your business becomes profitable when you are just starting. It is estimated to take two to three years for a business to be profitable on average. When a company begins to make a profit depends on how high it's start-up costs are. The number of years for profitability vary depending on the type of business you invest in and the capital invested. The more capital a business needs upfront to provide it's products or services and the higher it's salaries, the longer it will take for a company to become profitable. That's why it's best to minimize your investment; put more time into building the business, also known as sweat equity.

Chapter 3: Introduction To The Concept Of Money Management

The key to successful money management is developing and following a personal financial plan. Creating a financial plan will help you save money, feel good about your progress, and make appropriate decisions. A written financial plan is far more effective than one that's in your head. This includes the forms of payments you accept from your customers, where you put your money, how you pay your bills, and how you pay the money you owe. Learning the value of money at an early age will shape your life quality and help you stand out.

Money management covers the way you handle money. This includes how you take money from your customers, where you put your money, how you pay your bills, and how you pay your debts. Businesses need to make sure the money they take in is safe and managed properly. You must be aware of the proper way of managing money and the benefits of paying off debt, earning interest from investments, and other ways to use money. Businesses need to make sure the money they earn is secure. You also need to make sure you have controls to ensure the money your business receives reaches the bank. If you sell 100 units of your product and the selling price is $1.00, you need to have controls to make sure the $100.00 is received and deposited at the bank. If your cash sales do not balance with your bank deposit, you need to reconcile the difference. Treat the money you take in very carefully and make sure you use it wisely.

Paying yourself a salary

Some business owners pay themselves a salary. This salary is the income that you can use for your savings and lifestyle. Saving provides a safety net for life's uncertainties. Emergency savings funds should have enough money to cover about three months of expenses. Your expenses may be low, but you may have business expenses that you may need to cover if the business takes a downturn. Many entrepreneurs choose not to take a salary. Instead, they reinvest any profit back into the business. This allows the company to grow at a rapid rate.

Watch your costs and expenses

Keeping track of your expenses gives you a strong sense of where your money goes and can help you reach your financial goals. Doing this allows you to see what costs you can cut and which ones bring in the most revenue (or money into the business). For example, if you know that you spend a lot of money on advertising online, each $1 you spend on advertising brings an additional $5 in revenue. You may want to consider more advertising.

Proper ways to minimize taxes
Paying Taxes
As your business grows and becomes profitable, you'll have to pay taxes on that profit. The best thing about owning a business is that you'll have more tax benefits than most adults. You'll also be able to reduce your tax liability by deducting expenses that are necessary for your business. Such as a cell phone or household internet. Being a kid does not mean that you're exempt from paying taxes. Just as your business is required to be registered and licensed, payment of taxes is also necessary. There are federal, state, and local taxes that must be paid by a small business.

2. Maximize Tax Credits
As opposed to a tax deduction, a tax credit can lower your taxes dollar for dollar. A tax credit will reduce the amount of taxes you must pay. The government uses tax credits to encourage taxpayers to engage in certain activities or to grant tax relief. The IRS gives the following types of credits: earned income credit, first-time homebuyer credit, child and dependent care credit, adoption credit, education credit, and retirement savings contributions credit. The IRS adds new tax credits every year.

Chapter 4: Keys To Growing A Business

Moving your business from a start-up into a growing entity is a whole new adventure, one that can be both exhilarating and downright scary. How you will grow the company not only depends upon what you want from it now but also upon what you want from it in the long run

Focus On Customer Service And Communication Skills

Customer service is how you treat your customers before, during, and after a sale, i.e., the services a business offers to it's customers, especially when buying consumer goods, such as a computer and car. Customer service includes the initial buying, questions about a product, repair and replacement service, extended guarantees, regular communications of information, telephone and email follow-up, and complaint handling. The level of customer service dramatically affects customers' thoughts about a company. Businesses strive to provide a service level that stands out and exceeds a customer's expectations. The companies that succeed with customer service understand what they are doing and are always looking for ways of exceeding a customer's expectations. Customer service's main goal should be to respond to a customer to leave a lasting positive impression. When you examine customer service, think of the little important things to people and how your business can address these areas. The following are tips to help you with your customer service.

Be Customer Driven

The most successful businesses focus on what their customers need and want. They reveal the truths about their marketplace. They understand what their most possible customer is like and how they think. They also understand who their customers are, where they are, what they buy, and why they buy. They match their products to the desires of their established customers and target customers.

Appeal to Emotions

Customers buy emotionally and justify logically. Everyone either wants to gain pleasure or avoid pain. Your product or service must eliminate anxiety or discomfort or enrich their business or personal life.

Focus On Your Target Market

Your target market is the customers who are most likely to buy from you. Once you know who you're target market is, focus your marketing efforts on those customers. Avoid the urge to be all things to all people, hoping to get a larger market slice. The target market is comprised of consumers to whom the products or services have the most appeal.

You can't be all things to all people. Focus on the market segment that has the highest probability of purchasing your product or service. Fit your product to exactly what those people are looking for. Position your product and message to your target market with laser precision; so that you are the best option they have. Your target market is the only market that matters to you. Seek to become remarkable and dominate it.

What Are Their Buying Behaviors
Buying Behavior is the decision process involved in buying and using products. Buyers are essential partners in the business world. Without them, the wheels of industry grind to a halt. They are the focus of successful marketing; their needs and wants are the reason for marketing. Without understanding buyer behavior, your offer cannot be tailored to a potential buyer's demands. Buyers choose where they spend their money from the list of competitive offerings available. Therefore, they are in control of the marketplace. Also, buying behavior indicates the set of decisions that a buyer makes while buying goods.

What Is The Best Way To Reach Them
Buying behavior is determined by recognizing and understanding the circumstances that impact your customers. You have the opportunity to develop a strategy, a marketing message in line with the needs of their target consumers. To

understand buying behavior, the following factors must be taken into consideration:

Cultural Factors

Culture can be defined as the values, beliefs, preferences, and tastes handed down from one generation to the next. Culture is the broadest environmental determinant of consumer behavior. Therefore, you need to understand it's role in decision making. You must also monitor trends to spot changes in cultural values —marketing strategies and business practices that work in one country, maybe offensive or ineffective elsewhere. Hence cultural differences are particularly significant and complex to understand for international marketers. Cultures are not homogeneous entities with universal values. Each culture includes numerous subcultures – groups with their distinct modes of behavior.

Social Factors

Every customer belongs to several social circles. These groups impact an individual's decisions. Group members are expected to comply with these norms. The difference in-group status and roles can also affect buying behavior. The surprising impact of groups and group norms on individual behavior is the Asch phenomenon because psychologist S.E. Asch first documented it. Discussions of the Asch phenomenon raise reference groups' subject – groups whose value structures and standards influence a person's behavior. Consumers usually try to coordinate their purchase behavior with their perceptions of the values of their reference groups.

Young adults are especially vulnerable to the influence of reference groups. They often base their buying decisions on outside forces:

> What is popular with their friends?
> What is fashionable and trendy?
> What is popular?
> What are their heroes and role models using?

In nearly every reference group, a select few members act as opinion leaders. They are the trendsetters who are likely to purchase new products before others in the group. They share their experiences and opinions via word of mouth. Other members' are then more likely to follow suit.

Closely related to reference groups is the concept of social class. A social class is an identifiable group of individuals who share similar values and behavior patterns different from those of other classes. These values and behavior patterns affect their purchase decisions.

Familial Factors

The family group is perhaps the most important determinant of consumer behavior because of the close, continuing interactions among family members. Like other groups, each family typically has norms of expected behavior, different roles, and standards for it's members. One family can have a history of medical doctors or lawyers. A member who decides to pursue a career in the arts; may be looked down upon. One family may have a history of musicians, and a member decides they want to be a lawyer. They could be looked down upon by the musicians in their family. In some families, the members-only buy luxury cars; if a family member decides to buy a more economical vehicle. They could be mocked or ridiculed by their family. Some people will never go against the norms of their family. It would be challenging to sell that person a product or service that goes against their standards.

Psychological Factors:
These factors consist of perception, motivation, attitude, and beliefs. Perception is an individual's interpretation of the information. New experiences bring changes to a person's behavior. As a result, new ideas and attitudes affect their normal buying behavior. Consumer's psychologically deal with past experiences and decisions. Motivation can push a customer to look online to research different options online. Perception makes consumers examine the security of the web site or the quality of the product. In this case, the seller has to give the customers the confidence to purchase their product.

Personality factors may drive consumers to ask themselves what kinds of web sites are best suited for their personal preferences. Personal preferences compel consumers to make a decision. The fourth one is attitude, and attitudes can change quickly; therefore, marketers focus on changing attitudes. For example, Mercedes won't try to convert Ford drivers to purchase their cars. That would be too high of a hurdle to overcome. They prefer to concentrate their resources on retaining their customers. Then, they'll look to convert BMW customers to become Mercedes owners.

The last factor is emotion; they may consider their previous experiences. The outcomes of previous decisions; affect future choices.

Marketing Factors:

There are hundreds of different ways for you to reach your target customer. Continuous exposure to advertising, emails, and social media leads. While marketing certainly includes selling and advertising encompasses much more. Marketing also involves analyzing consumer needs. At the same time, securing the information needed to produce goods or services that match buyer expectations. Creating and maintaining relationships with customers and suppliers.

Offer the Best Value

You must have the desire to be the best in the world at what you do. Your business is your real product and, you have to hold your product, service, support staff, and yourself to a high standard. Your products, services, and systems must match the perception laid out in your brochures, website, sales claims, etc. You must be able to deliver on your promise. Everyone wants the best deal, that is, the best value. Your Unique Value Proposition (UVP) is derived from the quality you bring to the market and must set you apart from your competitors. Some companies use price as their UVP, but they are also the most vulnerable; because they will always be cheaper. It's best to set your company apart in ways that can't be duplicated.

Communicate a Powerful Message
Your marketing message—the "value proposition" and the "sensory package" (words, colors, logos, printed materials, etc.)—must explain how your offering will take away pain or improve their lives better than anyone else can. People buy benefits not features. For example, think of your favorite candy. You don't buy it because of the ingredients (feature) that are in it; you buy it because of the way it tastes (benefit).

Communicate a clear, powerful message that shows why you are unbeatable; there is power in clarity. Quantify, compare, or demonstrate your advantage or claims. Avoid the mindless fluff. Get real! Business philosopher Jim Rohn described a three-step process to be a master communicator. They are as follow:

Have something good to say (Have genuine positivity)

Know what to say (Be knowledgable)

Read the body language of your audience (People say more with their body than they do with their mouth)

Well-chosen words mixed with measured emotion (Match their energy)

Find Cost-Effective Channels

You have to find the most cost-effective marketing channels (internet, social media, word of mouth, google ads, etc.) to get your message to the targeted customers who need and want your product. The most effective marketing campaigns are multifaceted, combining two or more strategies. The best and most profitable marketing method is to have a great product or service. Sell that product to someone, provide excellent customer service to them. Have them become repeat customers or refer their friends or family to your service. Overall, it's expensive to obtain a new customer; but once someone buys from you. The likely hood they'll buy again increases dramatically; they are also more likely to spend exponentially more. That is why it's essential to take good care of your customers. While constantly marketing for new customers.

Bringing The Best Product Or Service To Market

Once you have one successful product, you can add more products to your product line. Each product line is an additional revenue stream. You could bundle them together as special deals to generate extra revenue. Apple is said to have 30 revenue streams. The more revenue streams you have, the more likely you will avoid entrepreneurship's ups and downs. My media company has over 25 books in our catalog. Some books sell better than others; others don't sell at all. The ones that sell the most, I double down and expand the product line for that book. One book becomes a softcover book, an e-book, a hardcover book, and ant sell audiobook. I'll then use that book as a source to gain repeat customers. For the ones that don't sell, I'll look at ways to repackage them. The key is to keep a certain standard of quality with each successive product line. Prepare a short questionnaire or even just a few verbal questions to determine whether people are interested in the products or services you want to sell and how much they'd be willing to pay for them. For safety's sake, it may be best to survey adult friends, family members, and kids -- if you plan to sell to them -- instead of strangers

Figuring Out Who Your Customer Is And How To Sell To Them

When a business knows who it's loyal customers are, it can establish what characteristics those customers have and attract more customers like them. Meet the needs of larger numbers of customers as the business grows. You only need 1,000 loyal fans to make a $100,000 in income. Yup, if $1,000 people buy one product at $100 each, you've just earned $100,000 in revenue.

Chapter 5: Types Of Business Entities

One of the most important decisions to make when establishing a new business is the entity you choose for your company. This chapter will provide an overview of the different business entities. To get an in-depth look into the business entity you choose, it's best to do your research and possibly contact an attorney. You're probably wondering, what is a business entity?

A business entity is established by an individual or group of individuals to manage and engage in business activities. If you have an accountant or legal advisor in your family or circle of influence, this is an excellent opportunity to ask for their input on this matter. An attorney or accountant you already know will be so impressed that you're asking such thought-provoking questions. They'll probably answer any question that you have. You can also ask your parents for their advice, or ask if they know someone who can help. This is also an excellent time to research with your parents. Remember the power of Youtube University.

We'll now take a look at the different options to structure your business:

1. Sole Proprietorship.
A sole proprietorship entity saves money, time, and is the easiest way to start a business. This is the simplest way to set up a business; if you don't choose a corporate structure, it will be a sole proprietorship by default. In a sole proprietorship,

you'll make all the business decisions and earns all the profits. You're personally accountable for all of the debts incurred by the business. You have unlimited liability in the event of an accident; if you're under 18, this liability can become your parent's liability. This liability can extend to your parents or guardians as well. A sole proprietorship may be operated under any name, and it should register it's tradename. Therefore, your parent may decide to register your business in their name.

A sole proprietorship can only last as long as the life of the sole proprietor. All income and expenses from the sole proprietorship flow directly to the sole proprietor so does all liability. The sole proprietor is personally accountable for their deliberate acts and omission of their employees. All properties, business and personal, of the sole proprietor are subject to their creditors' declarations. Sole proprietorships are suitable for kids starting up a service type business without employees. A sole proprietorship allows you to dive into your business with little to no expenses. Once you hire employees or take on certain liabilities, things change. This is the point that exposes where le proprietorships don't have the protection of other entities.

Partnership
Unlike the sole proprietorship, a partnership is more sophisticated both to set up and to run. It requires an understanding between at least two individuals engaging in

activities with the end goal of making a profit. There are benefits to a partnership — such as the pooled resources of the partners. In a partnership agreement, the partnership will be supervised by the partners; all partners can administer it in the partnership name.

Partners generally transfer money or investments to the partnership in trade for some ownership of the entity. If the partners approve, new partners may enter the partnership by transferring cash or assets. An existing partner may trade all or a percentage of their partnership interest to the incoming partner. Someone can also obtain a partnership interest in trade for services. Let's say you want to start a landscaping business, but you have no experience in cutting and maintaining a lawn. However, you have enough money to invest in a lawnmower and all the necessary tools needed to start the business. Your best friend has been helping his uncle with his landscaping business for the last two years. This is the perfect set up for a partnership! You invested financially. At the same time, he provides the experience and the ability to do most of the work.

Partners are responsible for self-employment taxes. Partnerships are pass-through entities. However, the partnership will have an EIN and prepare tax returns. All income or losses of the partnership flow through to the individual partners to be documented on their tax returns. Partner profits and losses are allocated in agreement with their pro-rata share (i.e., two partners usually share profits 50%-

50%). Partnerships are afforded enormous flexibility in that regard and may give rise to unique tax benefits.

Overall, partnerships contribute to a significant amount of economic and administrative flexibility. Income is taxed in the same way as a sole proprietor, but partnerships also have the same disadvantage as a sole proprietor. Namely, the partners do not enjoy liability protection, and partnership creditors may seize their assets. When creating a partnership, make sure to talk about finances, expectations, and even an exit strategy. An exit strategy allows your partnerships to decide when, how, and under what circumstances it will end. Doing so ahead a time removes issues down the road and people getting selective amnesia

Corporations

These business entities are a bit more complicated. In contrast to sole ownerships and partnerships, organizations have a legal identity separate from the owners, partners, and investors. Otherwise called a Limited Company, it is a legal entity independent of it's members (owners). Every investor's risk is restricted to the amount they invested. A lender with a case against the organization's assets can only make an investor responsible for the loan portion, equal to or lesser than each partner's original investment. Under certain circumstances, investors might be held liable for debts against the corporation.

A Board of Directors generally manages a corporation, consisting of a minimum of three persons. The owners of the corporation are it's stockholders. Stockholders of a corporation are those individuals who have invested cash or other assets in acquiring an ownership interest (stock) in the corporation. As stockholders of the corporation, they are charged with electing a Board of Directors and making decisions on significant corporate actions. Stockholders do not (except in the case of a close corporation, which will be discussed below) manage the business. That job is left to the Board of Directors. No stockholder, individually, has the right to bind the corporation to agreements or commitments. As an owner, you'll need to own at least 1% of the corporation's stocks. The remaining 99% can stay in the corporation for future use. In the beginning, you'll probably hold all positions in the board of directors. It's important to point out that you need to talk with a parent or attorney. A corporation remains valid until it dissolved under state law.

C Corporation

C corporation are subject to subchapter C of the Internal Revenue Code. Distinct from partnerships, corporations may have only one owner and can only be established by formally filing paperwork with your local Secretary Of State's office. Rules for filing and filing fees apply here; there are also certain record-keeping and yearly reporting regulations.

S Corporation

S corporation are ruled by subchapter S of the Internal Revenue Code. S corporation offers many of the same benefits of C corporations, encompassing liability protection. S corporations are different in that they are taxed like partnerships. They allow pass-through taxation and special allocations among owners. Which can trigger double taxation, which is when you pay tax bills on the same income. There are also constraints as to ownership, as well as restrictions regarding the distribution of company revenues.

Limited Liability Company

A Limited Liability Company (LLC) has some of the best characteristics of corporations and partnerships. It is, practically, a partnership with limited liability protection.

The LLC,
(i) does not restrict ownership to specific individuals,
(ii) is designed to allow pass-through taxation and special allocations among owners, and
(iii) limits every owners' liability to the extent of their capital contributed to the business.

For a small business that is new and doesn't have a ton of liability concerns, the sole proprietorship and partnership entities are probably the best options. However, in expanding the business, a limited liability company and private corporations are better options. I've had several companies held under different types of entities. For me, the LLC has proven to be the most beneficial.

Chapter 6: Customer Service & Effective Marketing

Now, to the fun part! Marketing is the effort that you put forth to connect your product or service with a potential customer. Marketing affects many different activities, such as sales, advertising, customer service, product development, pricing, discounts, reputation, distribution, promotions, and much more. Marketers act as the company's parent, guiding many aspects of the company's life. Marketing is the process of planning and executing the distribution of ideas.

One aspect of marketing is advertising. Advertising is paid communication to build awareness of a particular brand, product, or service.

To create awareness for your product, you want to break through all the clutter in your market by clearly communicating your brand's name. It's essential features and benefits in a way that will make people want to buy your product. Effective advertising gets someone to purchase your product. As stated before, acquiring new customers can be tedious and expensive. Once you have a customer, you want to provide excellent service, combined with a great product. This will get your new customer to purchase other products from you. As well as recommend that their friends and family members do business with your company. This is what will allow your company to scale (grow). We'll now take a look at the different types of advertising.

Word of mouth

Word-of-mouth advertising is the most effective and cost-efficient marketing strategy, also known as social proof. Online reviews about a product or service are considered social proof. Most people check the reviews on a product before they'll purchase something online.

Word of mouth is any positive or negative statement made by customers' experiences about a product or company. Word of Mouth is the communication between two people about a business, product, or service.

Social Media

Creating an engaging profile on your preferred social media network has proven to steer consumers towards your business. Social media accounts can provide a sense of community for your customers and potential customers. It's a cost-effective way to increase visibility with consumers. This exposure also means that anyone can voice their opinion about your product or company. If the opinion is favorable, it can be beneficial to the company, but an unfavorable remark could drive away business. Facebook, Instagram, Twitter, and other social networks provide a way to build a following for your business as you post updates, photos, and videos to showcase your products and services.

Overall, social media is too powerful of a tool to ignore. Not too long ago, companies paid millions for the same exposure that you can have on Instagram for free. So you should use the power of social media to create awareness of your business and get people talking about your business.

Society is dominated by the internet, online services, mobile devices, and related technologies. Naturally, marketing had to follow this lead, and as a result, the new world of online marketing opened the door to all businesses across the globe. As stated earlier, online marketing allows small to medium-sized companies to compete with a large multinational company to market services and products. Online marketers can influence a customers' decision-making by engaging in traditional marketing tools; and delivering the proper online experience. Unlike traditional methods of advertising, such as television and radio, online marketing is more affordable.

Promotions

A promotion creates awareness and drives sales. Promotions communicate the brand benefits at the point of purchase while providing some incentive for consumers to buy. Social media is great for promotions; they motivate people to learn about your business. Usually, promotions have a catchy phrase and some kind of prize or incentive to buy a product. You see promotions all the time. It might be a toy in a cereal box or a chance to win something if you fill out a contest form. The idea is to reward and encourage you to buy a product. The reason this tactic is useful is that it compels someone to find out about your business. You then have the opportunity to persuade them to purchase your product or service. Once they make a purchase, your mission is to provide excellent customer service, assuming the product you sold them was a quality product. Now you have the chance to persuade them to make repeat sales. Remember, people are not only prone to purchase from you again. But they'll also be inclined to buy a more expensive item the more times they buy with you. They'll also refer their friends and family to you!

Referrals are the lifeline of a successful business – there's no better way of building sales than by increasing referrals. They are not only the number one source of new business; they're the best customer to have. You're piggybacking on the word of the person that referred them to your business. People like to make referrals – when we make a wise purchasing decision, we want to share it with others as a way of validating our good judgment and good fortune.

To get referrals, you have to ask for them! If you're talking to one of your customers, you might say:

"As you know, we do a lot of work with customers such as yourself; If you know of anyone you think we can help, would you be willing to introduce us?"

Almost every customer will say yes. Not all of them will follow through – but you've planted the seed! As kids, it is easier to persuade their friends and adults because of compassion - almost everyone wants to help an ambitious kid. You can also join a business referral group. Business referral groups bring business people together regularly, usually over breakfast or lunch, for the express purpose of generating business for each other. If you have people in your area who want to develop a personal referral network, this is an excellent place to start. You may need to participate in more than one group before you find the right fit. Make a plan to search for business clubs in your area.

Publicity
Publicity is coverage of your product or business in a news medium, such as newspapers, radio, television, online and social media. This is a hard thing for every company to do, but as a kid in business, you may be able to get a little more attention than most companies.

Public relations (P.R.) is the active pursuit of publicity for marketing purposes. If you can create good stories and communicate them to the media effectively, they might pick up the information and give you publicity. If you are successful in getting good publicity, it will help your business. Once people are aware of your business, your chance of converting them to customers improves significantly. This is also a great catalyst for social proof.

Networking
Do your networking with likeminded business people – it can be a cost-effective method of generating new leads. People tend to do business with people they know, like, and trust.

Networking helps to develop relationships that can help to obtain jobs and create business opportunities. Friendships that you develop—in school, activities, and neighborhoods—can help build a network. LinkedIn is an example of a professional networking platform that provides a way for you to establish and keep track of a network.

Chapter 6: Business & Financial Terminology

Now we'll look at the terminology you'll need to be familiar with as a budding entrepreneur:

Banking/Financial Acronyms

APR - Annual Percentage Rate, is a way of measuring the full cost a lender charges per year for funds. Typically associated with mortgages, loans, and credit cards, APR combines the total amount of interest payable and the cost of other fees, averaged over the term of the loan, and expressed as a percentage.

ARM - an adjustable-rate mortgage (ARM) is a type of mortgage in which the interest rate applied on the outstanding balance varies throughout the loan's life. With an adjustable-rate mortgage, the initial interest rate is fixed for a period of time. After this initial period of time, the interest rate resets periodically, at yearly or even monthly intervals. ARMs are also called variable-rate mortgages or floating mortgages. The interest rate for ARMs is reset based on a benchmark or index, plus an additional spread called an ARM margin.

CD - A certificate of deposit (CD) is a type of savings account usually issued by commercial banks, which restricts your access to the money you invest but offers much higher interest rates than those associated with regular savings accounts. The deposit gains value over an agreed-upon duration, but it could be subject to fees if withdrawn before the end of that time.

EFT - An electronic funds transfer system (EFTS) is a transfer system in which money can be transferred to business or individual accounts without requiring paper money to change hands. Electronic funds transfer systems are used for payroll payments, debit or credit transfers, mortgage payments, or other payments. Most financial institutions use electronic funds transfer systems

FDIC - The Federal Deposit Insurance Corporation (FDIC) is a U.S. government institution that provides deposit insurance against bank failure. The body was created during the Great Depression when the public had lost trust in the banking system. Before it's formation, a third of U.S. banks collapsed, leading to the loss of many depositors' funds. There was no guarantee on bank deposits other than the bank's stability, and only depositors who were quick enough to withdraw their money were lucky enough to retain it. The FDIC was established to maintain public confidence in the financial system and promote sound banking practices.

LOI - A letter of intent is an introductory letter to employers, businesses, or financial institutions you're interested in working with. Typically, a person would send a letter of intent to hiring managers or recruiters at a company that has not posted jobs relevant to their background. Although similar to a cover letter, a letter of intent provides less detail about a specific job. Instead, a letter of intent is designed to express your interest in working with an organization. An LOI may be required by a bank that you want to get a loan from. The LOI could be from a client that intends to hire you. In this case, the LOI shows proof of how your debt will be repaid.

MTD - Month-to-date is a period starting at the beginning of the current month and ending at the current date. Month-to-date is used in many contexts, mainly for recording activity results between a date and the beginning of the current month. In the context of finance, MTD is often provided in financial statements detailing a business entity's performance.

NAV - The net asset value (NAV) represents the net value of an entity. It is calculated as the total value of the entity's assets minus the full value of it's liabilities. Most commonly used in the context of a mutual fund or an exchange-traded fund (ETF), the NAV represents the fund's per share/unit price on a specific date or time. NAV is the price at which the shares/units of the funds registered with the U.S. Securities and Exchange Commission (SEC) are traded (invested or redeemed).

P&L - A profit and loss (P&L) statement is a financial report that summarizes a company's revenue, expenses, and profit. It gives investors and other interested parties an insight into how a company operates and whether it can generate a profit.

P/E ratio - The price-to-earnings ratio (P/E ratio) is the ratio for valuing a company that measures it's current share price relative to it's per-share earnings (EPS). The price-to-earnings ratio is also sometimes known as the price multiple or the earnings multiple.

QTD - Quarter-to-date (QTD) is a time interval that captures all relevant company activity that occurred between the beginning of the current quarter and the point at which the data was gathered later in the quarter. Quarter-to-date information is typically collected in situations when the entire quarterly period has not yet ended, and it can allow management to see how the quarter is shaping up

ROA - Return on assets (ROA) is an indicator of how profitable a company is relative to it's total assets. ROA gives a manager, investor, or analyst an idea of how efficient a company's management is at using it's assets to generate earnings. Return on assets is displayed as a percentage.

ROCE - Return On Capital Employed is a financial ratio that determines a company's profitability and the efficiency the capital is applied. A higher ROCE implies a more economical use of capital; the ROCE should be higher than the capital cost. If not, the company is less productive and inadequately building shareholder value.

ROE - Return on equity (ROE) is a measure of financial performance calculated by dividing net income by shareholders' equity. Because shareholders' equity is equal to a company's assets minus it's debt, ROE is considered the return on net assets. ROE is viewed as a measure of how effectively management uses a company's assets to determine profitability.

ROI - Return on Investment measures the gain or loss generated by an investment compared to it's initial cost. It allows the reader to gauge the efficiency and profitability of an investment and is often used to influence financial decisions, compare a company's profitability, and analyze investments

ROIC - Return on invested capital (ROIC) is a calculation used to assess a company's efficiency at allocating the capital under it's control to profitable investments. The return on invested capital ratio gives a sense of how well a company uses it'smoney to generate returns.

RONA - Return on net assets (RONA) is a measure of financial performance calculated as net profit divided by the sum of fixed assets and net working capital. Net profit is also called net income

ROS - Return on sales (ROS) is a measure of how efficiently a company turns sales into profit. ROS is calculated by dividing operating profit by net sales. ROS is only useful when comparing companies in the same line of business and of roughly the same size.

W.C. - Working capital, also known as net working capital (NWC), is the difference between a company's current assets. Such as cash, accounts receivable (your customer's unpaid bills), and inventories of raw materials and finished goods. Net operating working capital is a measure of a company's liquidity. It refers to the difference between current operating assets and current operating liabilities. In many cases, these calculations are the same and are derived from company cash, plus accounts receivable, plus inventories, less accounts payable, and less accrued expenses.

YTD - Year to date (YTD) refers to the period of time beginning the first day of the current calendar year or fiscal year up to the current date. YTD information is useful for analyzing business trends over time or comparing performance data to competitors or peers in the same industry. The acronym often modifies concepts such as investment returns, earnings, and net pay.

Entrepreneurial Terminology
LLC - A limited liability company is a separate and distinct legal entity. This means that an LLC can get a tax identification number, open a bank account, and do business, all under the business name.

C Corp - C corporation is a legal structure for a corporation in which the owners, or shareholders, are taxed separately from the entity. C corporations, the most prevalent of corporations, are also subject to corporate income taxation. The taxing of profits from the business is at both corporate and personal levels, creating a double taxation situation.

S Corp- S corporation, also known as an S subchapter, refers to a type of corporation that meets specific Internal Revenue Code requirements. The requirements give a corporation with 100 shareholders or less the benefit of incorporation while being taxed as a partnership. The corporation may pass income directly to shareholders and avoid double taxation.

CEO – The Chief Executive Officer is the highest-ranking executive in a company. Their primary responsibilities include making major corporate decisions, managing a company's overall operations and resources, acting as the main point of communication between the board of directors (the board) and corporate operations, and being the company's public face. The board elects a CEO, and it's shareholders.

CAO - Chief Accounting Officer is responsible for overseeing all accounting functions such as ledger accounts, financial statements, and cost control systems. Their focus includes regulatory compliance and practices and collaborating with the CFO, developing financial strategies.

CFO - Chief financial officer is a senior executive responsible for managing the financial actions of a company. The CFO's duties include tracking cash flow and financial planning, analyzing it's financial strengths and weaknesses, and proposing corrective actions.

CISA - Certified Information Systems Auditor - Certified Information Systems Auditor is a certification issued by ISACA (Information Systems Audit and Control Association) to people in charge of ensuring that an organization's I.T. and business systems are monitored, managed, and protected; the certification is presented after completion of a comprehensive testing and application process.

CMA - Certified Management Accountant- Certified Management Accountant is an accounting designation that signifies financial accounting and strategic management expertise. This certification builds on financial accounting proficiency by adding management skills to make strategic business decisions based on financial data.

CMO - Chief Marketing Officer is for activities in an organization that have to create, communicate, and deliver offerings that have value for customers, clients, or business partners.

COO - Chief Operating Officer (COO) is a senior executive tasked with overseeing a business's day-to-day administrative and operational functions. The COO typically reports directly to the chief executive officer (CEO) and is considered second in the chain of command.

CPA - Certified Public Accountant is a designation given by the American Institute of Certified Public Accountants (AICPA) to individuals that pass the Uniform CPA Examination and meet the education and experience requirements. The CPA designation helps enforce professional standards in the accounting industry. Other countries have certifications equivalent to the CPA designation, notably, the chartered accountant (C.A.) designation.

CPP - Certified Payroll Professional is a financial clerk specializing in payroll who has earned a professional certification from the American Payroll Association, a prominent industry organization. Payroll clerks keep track of employee hours and payroll information, and they compile the data to prepare paychecks of all employees. Before sending them out, payroll clerks verify that all paychecks are accurate, and they make adjustments if necessary.

CSO - Chief Security Officer is the company executive responsible for the security of personnel, physical assets, and information in both physical and digital form. This position's importance has increased in the age of information technology (I.T.) as it has become easier to steal sensitive company information.

CTO - Chief Technology Officer is the executive in charge of an organization's technological needs, and it's research and development (R & D). Also known as a chief technical officer, this individual examines the short- and long-term needs of an organization and utilizes capital to make investments designed to help the organization reach it's objectives. The CTO usually reports directly to the chief executive officer (CEO) of the firm.

THE IMPORTANCE OF CREDIT

In most cases, credit can only be extended to individuals 18 years or older. If you're under the age of 18 this section will only be for informational purposes. You can choose to come back at a later time. So that you can focus on starting and building your business.

Moving forward, credit play an important role in the life of both the business and the business owner. Credit is an agreement to repay debt incurred from borrowed funds; used in paying for goods and services. The sale of most commodities is accomplished through the extension of credit. Without a good credit history, getting a loan, a credit card or even an apartment may pose difficulties.

Personal Credit

Utilizing personal credit to finance products or services for your business, can put your personal resources in danger. In the event that the business comes up short or encounters a cash shortage, and can't repay it's obligations. The lender will can come after YOU, as you will be personally responsible for the fees incurred by the business

Fico Scores

Your credit score is a 3 digit number used by creditors to perform a risk assessment before extending credit. FICO scores are the most utilized financial assessments. FICO is also the most commonly used method of scoring personal credit. There are three major credit bureaus—Experian, TransUnion, and Equifax. Creditors use FICO scores to help them rapidly, reliably, and equitably assess potential borrowers' credit risk. FICO score is a numbering system established as a result of your personal creditworthiness; based on previous and present usage of credit. To know more about FICO score and what their fico score is, you should visit http://www.myfico.com.

Business Credit

Like personal credit, there is also business credit. Business credit is one of the most important factors in growing your business. It is the credit that is obtained in a Business Name. Different agencies calculate business credit, and each of the agencies has a way of doing it's own analysis, but generally, the score ranges from 0 to 100. The higher the number, the lower the calculated risk. The circumstances that influence business credit may include public records, like liens or bankruptcies, credit, like outstanding balances and payment habits, and demographic information, such as business size and years on record. Very strong business credit can influence the growth of a business. Business creditworthiness is measured by a Paydex score. To check your business' paydex score, you should visit http://www.dnb.com.

Chapter 7: Successful Kid Entrepreneurs

1. Jack Bonneau is the kid who started a lemonade business at the age of eight, with the help of his father, Jack ambitiously traded cups of lemonade at a local farmers' market.
He amassed up to $2,000 and earned a nice profit of about $900. He proceeded to broaden his lemonade business and developed a website. He now does his lemonade sales at three more farmers' markets .

2. Cory Nieves (15yr old) – CEO and founder of Mr Cory's Cookies. At just 6 years old, he resolved to start selling hot cocoa and cookies outside a local pizzeria to raise enough money to buy a car for himself and his mom. Although the business had seen a lot of ups and downs, Cory made his big break when ABC News and the Huffington Post got wind of his story. He was helped onto the Ellen DeGeneres show where he and his mother were gifted with $10,000 and a brand-new 2015 Ford Escape customized with his company logo.

3. Moziah Bridges (19yr old) – CEO and founder of Mo's Bows. Moziah's fashion sense led him to start his bow tie business at the age of nine. Mo's bows handmade bow ties is a Memphis-based and family run business. With the help of his mother, and grandmother, who is a retired seamstress, moziah began selling bow ties on his website (mosbowsmemphis.com) and in Memphis retail stores.

4. Taylor Rosenthal (17yrs old) – CEO and founder of RecMed First Aid Kits. The idea for RecMed, a vending machine that

dispenses first aid materials such as Band-Aids, hydrocortisone pads, and gauze, was brought up by Taylor when he was in eighth grade in Opelika, Alabama.

5. Mikaila Ulmer (14yrs old) – CEO and founder of Me & The Bees Lemonade. Mikaila started her lemonade business in Austin, texas. Her lemonade business, bees lemonade, is said to worth over 11 million dollars in whole foods deal. Her lemonade is sold in over 1500 stores.

6. Callum Daniel (10yrs old) – CEO and founder of iCodeRobots. Callum became aware of robots for the first time at the age of four, after a holiday to Butlins where he was captivated by a robot named Titan. Since then, he became obsessed with finding out how Titian worked, which led to Callum's mum buying him his own robot soon afterwards. As one of the youngest CEO's of our time, Callum runs his own company called iCodeRobots, which he started so that he could share his love of robotics and coding with other children.

7. Kenan Pala (Age 16) — Kids4Community. Kenan is a volunteer and a student who is passionate about helping others in need.

8. Langston Whitlock (Age 17) — Cofounder and CIO of Safe trip. Langston coded his first anonymous messaging app in JavaScript at 12. SAFETRIP is an healthcare based ridesharing app which enables users to book non-emergency medical transport (NEMT) and emergency medical transport (EMT) Users can schedule rides or travel on demand, saving users both time and money. It's patented technology allows users to

pay for rides with insurance, debit, or credit cards. The platform, which has $2M in funding, offers real-time ride tracking and ratings systems for both users and drivers to ensure safety and quality.

9. John Feinsibler (Age 17) — Gimkit. Josh birthed Gimkit when he was brainstorming for a new project. He improved on the idea and execution of Kahoot, which is another learning game.
Gimkit is a live quiz learning application that enables teachers create "kits" that awards students when they have learned and memorized concepts

10. Jeremy Miller (Age 19) — Void longboards. He is a 19 year old entrepreneur and marketing guru who started his skateboard manufacturing, Void Longboards, when he was only 16 and after 8 months of testing different social media strategies to grow online, he hit over 100M organic impressions on content

About the Author

Maurice Sanders is a serial entrepreneur. He is an eternal optimist and has a knack for adventure. Having seen his fair share of ups and downs in life, he continues to develop businesses and jumpstart new ventures. He possesses a flair for teaching entrepreneur skills and has also taught at the Chicago Urban League. Maurice holds a bachelor's degree in computer science and marketing from Northern Illinois University.

A couple of his favorite quotes include:

"Success is the progressive step towards a worthy goal"

"You will be the same person in five years as you are today except for the people you meet and the books you read"

When he is not working, he is sculpting or coaching new entrepreneurs into launching successful business ventures. He also enjoys travelling and thinking about his next journey in life.

If you're looking for help in reaching your life or business goals. Contact Maurice directly at maurice@mauricethefirst.com to invest in one on coaching. You can also follow us on Instagram @mauricethe1st. To get access to free resources to help grow your business while saving time and money visit http://www.mauricethefirst.com

Check out Maurice's other books:

6 Figure Trucking: You're Only One Decision Away From $150K

6 Figure Entrepreneur: Start A $150,000 Business In 21 Days

To help us continue to bring the best books to the market. Please leave a review on the platform that you bought this book about what you gained from reading these pages. This also gives new readers the opportunity to see what knowledge other readers gained from this book

REFERENCE

Consumer buying behavior towards online shopping; lakshmi. S 1 m.phil research scholar, department of management studies, manonmaniam sundarnar/international journal of research,granthaalayah/http://www.granthaalayah.com/university, tirunelveli, india

Effective strategies for personal money management
Factors influencing consumer behavior/pinki rani; corresponding author, institute of law kurukshetra, university kurukshetra, india

Modern marketing practice; k.sudhakar, s.r.guru prasath, v.ashok kumar/iosr journal of business and management (iosr-jbm)/e-issn : 2278-487x, p-issn : 2319-7668, pp 34-37/www.iosrjournals.org

Word-of-mouth marketing from a global perspective by eda sirma/ iscte business school

Word of mouth and it's impact on marketing ; by fatima naz/department of business studies, kinnaird college for women lahore, 93-jail road lahore, Pakistan

The kids' guide to business/ second edition/ introducing, preparing, and launching kids into business; by jeff m. Brown

10 simple steps to grow the perfect business/an entrepreneur's' guide; by ron carroll

Strategic planning & goal setting assessments: strategic planning & goal setting.
Teaching kids business: why, what, when, where, how & impact by jeff m. Brown.

57 ways to grow your business;bright ideas for the serious entrepreneur;the 2020 group.

50 small business ideas for kids/www.smallbiztrends.com.

Ways to minimize income tax/https://finance.zacks.com/ways-minimize-income-tax.

Ten ways to lower your taxes; www.tax.findlaw.com/federal-taxes/ten-ways-to-lower-your-taxes.

11 examples of target customers; www.simplicable.com/new/target-customer
13 ways to help your kid ceo start their own business; www.redtri.com/how-parents-can-help-kids-start-their-own-business/amp/

Chief operating officer; www.investopedia.com/terms/c/coo.asp

Chief financial officer; www.investopedia.com/terms/c/cfo.asp

How long does it take a business to be profitable; www.freshbooks.com
WWW.FORBES. COM